No Treason: The Constitution of No Authority

Lysander Spooner

CONTENTS

Chapter 1

The Constitution has no inherent authority or obligation. It has no authority or obligation at all, unless as a contract between man and man. And it does not so much as even purport to be a contract between persons now existing. It purports, at most, to be only a contract between persons living eighty years ago. [This essay was written in 1869.] And it can be supposed to have been a contract then only between persons who had already come to years of discretion, so as to be competent to make reasonable and obligatory contracts. Furthermore, we know, historically, that only a small portion even of the people then existing were consulted on the subject, or asked, or permitted to express either their consent or dissent in any formal manner. Those persons, if any, who did give their consent formally, are all dead now. Most of them have been dead forty, fifty, sixty, or seventy years. AND THE CONSTITUTION, SO FAR AS IT WAS THEIR CONTRACT, DIED WITH THEM. They had no natural power or right to make it obligatory upon their children. It is not only plainly impossible, in the nature of things, that they COULD bind their posterity, but they did not even attempt to bind them. That is to say, the instrument does not purport to be an agreement between any body but "the people" THEN existing; nor does it, either expressly or impliedly, assert any right, power, or disposition, on their part, to bind anybody but themselves. Let us see. Its language is:

We, the people of the United States (that is, the people THEN EXISTING in the United States), in order to form a more perfect union, insure domestic tranquility, provide for the common defense, promote the general welfare, and secure the blessings of liberty to ourselves

AND OUR POSTERITY, do ordain and establish this Constitution for the

United States of America.

It is plain, in the first place, that this language, AS AN AGREEMENT, purports to be only what it at most really was, viz., a contract between the people then existing; and, of necessity, binding, as a contract, only upon those then existing. In the second place, the language neither expresses nor implies that they had any right or power, to bind their "posterity" to live under it. It does not say that their "posterity" will, shall, or must live under it. It only says, in effect, that their hopes and motives in adopting it were that it might prove useful to their posterity, as well as to themselves, by promoting their union, safety, tranquility, liberty, etc.

Suppose an agreement were entered into, in this form:

We, the people of Boston, agree to maintain a fort on Governor's Island, to protect ourselves and our posterity against invasion.

This agreement, as an agreement, would clearly bind nobody but the people then existing. Secondly, it would assert no right, power, or disposition, on their part, to compel their "posterity" to maintain such a fort. It would only indicate that the supposed welfare of their posterity was one of the motives that induced the original parties to enter into the agreement.

When a man says he is building a house for himself and his posterity, he does not mean to be understood as saying that he has any thought of binding them, nor is it to be inferred that he is so foolish as to imagine that he has any right or power to bind them, to live in it. So far as they are concerned, he only means to be understood as saying that his hopes and motives, in building it, are that they, or at least some of them, may find it for their happiness to live in it.

So when a man says he is planting a tree for himself and his posterity, he does not mean to be understood as saying that he has any thought of compelling them, nor is it to be inferred that he is such a simpleton as to imagine that he has any right or power to compel them, to eat the fruit. So far as they are concerned, he only means to say that his hopes and motives, in planting the tree, are that its fruit may be agreeable to them.

So it was with those who originally adopted the Constitution. Whatever may have been their personal intentions, the legal meaning of their language, so far as their "posterity" was concerned, simply was, that their hopes and motives, in entering into the agreement, were that it might prove useful and acceptable to their posterity; that it might promote their union, safety, tranquility, and welfare; and that it might tend "to secure to them the blessings of liberty." The language does not assert nor at all imply, any right, power, or disposition, on the part of the original parties to the agreement, to compel their "posterity" to live under it. If they had intended to bind their posterity to live under it, they should have said that their objective was, not "to secure to them the blessings of liberty," but to make slaves of them; for if their "posterity" are bound to live under it, they are nothing less than the slaves of their foolish, tyrannical, and dead grandfathers.

It cannot be said that the Constitution formed "the people of the United States," for all time, into a corporation. It does not speak of "the people" as a corporation, but as individuals. A corporation does not describe itself as "we," nor as "people," nor as "ourselves." Nor does a corporation, in legal language, have any "posterity." It supposes itself to have, and speaks of itself as having, perpetual existence, as a single individuality.

Moreover, no body of men, existing at any one time, have the power to create a perpetual corporation. A corporation can become practically perpetual only by the voluntary accession of new members, as the old ones die off. But for this voluntary accession of new members, the corporation necessarily dies with the death of those who originally composed it.

Legally speaking, therefore, there is, in the Constitution, nothing that professes or attempts to bind the "posterity" of those who established it.

If, then, those who established the Constitution, had no power to bind, and did not attempt to bind, their posterity, the question arises, whether their posterity have bound themselves. If they have done so, they can have done so in only one or both of these two ways, viz., by voting, and paying taxes.

Chapter 2

Let us consider these two matters, voting and tax paying, separately. And first of voting.

All the voting that has ever taken place under the Constitution, has been of such a kind that it not only did not pledge the whole people to support the Constitution, but it did not even pledge any one of them to do so, as the following considerations show.

1. In the very nature of things, the act of voting could bind nobody but the actual voters. But owing to the property qualifications required, it is probable that, during the first twenty or thirty years under the Constitution, not more than one-tenth, fifteenth, or perhaps twentieth of the whole population (black and white, men, women, and minors) were permitted to vote. Consequently, so far as voting was concerned, not more than one-tenth, fifteenth, or twentieth of those then existing, could have incurred any obligation to support the Constitution.

At the present time [1869], it is probable that not more than one-sixth of the whole population are permitted to vote. Consequently, so far as voting is concerned, the other five-sixths can have given no pledge that they will support the Constitution.

2. Of the one-sixth that are permitted to vote, probably not more than two-thirds (about one-ninth of the whole population) have usually voted. Many never vote at all. Many vote only once in two, three, five, or ten years, in periods of great excitement.

No one, by voting, can be said to pledge himself for any longer period than that for which he votes. If, for example, I vote for an officer who is to hold his office for only a year, I cannot be said to have thereby pledged myself to support the government beyond that term. Therefore, on the ground of actual voting, it probably cannot be said that more than one-ninth or one-eighth, of the whole population are usually under any pledge to support the Constitution. [In recent years, since 1940, the number of voters in elections has usually fluctuated between one-third and two-fifths of the populace.]

3. It cannot be said that, by voting, a man pledges himself to support the Constitution, unless the act of voting be a perfectly voluntary one on his part. Yet the act of voting cannot properly be called a voluntary one on the part of any very large number of those who do vote. It is rather a measure of necessity imposed upon them by others, than one of their own choice. On this point I repeat what was said in a former number, viz.:

"In truth, in the case of individuals, their actual voting is not to be taken as proof of consent, EVEN FOR THE TIME BEING. On the contrary, it is to be considered that, without his consent having even been asked a man finds himself environed by a government that he cannot resist; a government that forces him to pay money, render service, and forego the exercise of many of his natural rights, under peril of weighty punishments. He sees, too, that other men practice this tyranny over him by the use of the ballot. He sees further, that, if he will but use the ballot himself, he has some chance of relieving himself from this tyranny of others, by subjecting them to his own. In short, he finds himself, without his consent, so situated that, if he use the ballot, he may become a master; if he does not use it, he must become a slave. And he has no other alternative than these two. In self-defence, he attempts the former. His case is analogous to that of a man who has been forced into battle, where he must either kill others, or be killed himself. Because, to save his own life in battle, a man takes the lives of his opponents, it is not to be inferred that the battle is one of his own choosing. Neither in contests with the ballot - which is a mere substitute for a bullet - because, as his only chance of self-preservation, a man uses a ballot, is it to be inferred that the contest is one into which he voluntarily entered; that he voluntarily set up all his own natural rights, as a stake against those of others, to be lost or won by the mere power of numbers. On the contrary, it is to be considered that, in an exigency into which he had been forced by others, and in which no other means of self-defence offered, he, as a matter of necessity, used the only one that was left to him.

"Doubtless the most miserable of men, under the most oppressive government in the world, if allowed the ballot, would use it, if they could see any chance of thereby meliorating their condition. But it would not, therefore, be a legitimate inference that the government itself, that crushes them, was one which they had voluntarily set up, or even consented to.

"Therefore, a man's voting under the Constitution of the United States, is not to be taken as evidence that he ever freely assented to the Constitution, EVEN FOR THE TIME BEING. Consequently we have no proof that any very large portion, even of the actual voters of the United States, ever really and voluntarily consented to the Constitution, EVEN FOR THE TIME BEING. Nor can we ever have such proof, until every man is left perfectly free to consent, or not, without thereby subjecting himself or his property to be disturbed or injured by others."

As we can have no legal knowledge as to who votes from choice, and who from the necessity thus forced upon him, we can have no legal knowledge, as to any particular individual, that he voted from choice; or, consequently, that by voting, he consented, or pledged himself, to support the government. Legally speaking, therefore, the act of voting utterly fails to pledge ANY ONE to support the government. It utterly fails to prove that the government rests upon the voluntary support of anybody. On general principles of law and reason, it cannot be said that the government has any voluntary supporters at all, until it can be distinctly shown who its voluntary supporters are.

4. As taxation is made compulsory on all, whether they vote or not, a large proportion of those who vote, no doubt do so to prevent their own money being used against themselves; when, in fact, they would have gladly abstained from voting, if they could thereby have saved themselves from taxation alone, to say nothing of being saved from all the other usurpations and tyrannies of the government. To take a man's property without his consent, and then to infer his consent because he attempts, by voting, to prevent that property from being used to his injury, is a very insufficient proof of his consent to support the Constitution. It is, in fact, no proof at all. And as we can have no legal knowledge as to who the particular individuals are, if there are any, who are willing to be taxed for the sake of voting, we can have no legal knowledge that any particular

individual consents to be taxed for the sake of voting; or, consequently, consents to support the Constitution.

5. At nearly all elections, votes are given for various candidates for the same office. Those who vote for the unsuccessful candidates cannot properly be said to have voted to sustain the Constitution. They may, with more reason, be supposed to have voted, not to support the Constitution, but specially to prevent the tyranny which they anticipate the successful candidate intends to practice upon them under color of the Constitution; and therefore may reasonably be supposed to have voted against the Constitution itself. This supposition is the more reasonable, inasmuch as such voting is the only mode allowed to them of expressing their dissent to the Constitution.

6. Many votes are usually given for candidates who have no prospect of success. Those who give such votes may reasonably be supposed to have voted as they did, with a special intention, not to support, but to obstruct the exection of, the Constitution; and, therefore, against the Constitution itself.

7. As all the different votes are given secretly (by secret ballot), there is no legal means of knowing, from the votes themselves, who votes for, and who votes against, the Constitution. Therefore, voting affords no legal evidence that any particular individual supports the Constitution. And where there can be no legal evidence that any particular individual supports the Constitution, it cannot legally be said that anybody supports it. It is clearly impossible to have any legal proof of the intentions of large numbers of

men, where there can be no legal proof of the intentions of any particular one of them.

8. There being no legal proof of any man's intentions, in voting, we can only conjecture them. As a conjecture, it is probable, that a very large proportion of those who vote, do so on this principle, viz., that if, by voting, they could but get the government into their own hands (or that of their friends), and use its powers against their opponents, they would then willingly support the Constitution; but if their opponents are to have the power, and use it against them, then they would NOT willingly support the Constitution.

In short, men's voluntary support of the Constitution is doubtless, in most cases, wholly contingent upon the question whether, by means of the Constitution, they can make themselves masters, or are to be made slaves.

Such contingent consent as that is, in law and reason, no consent at all.

9. As everybody who supports the Constitution by voting (if there are any such) does so secretly (by secret ballot), and in a way to avoid all personal responsibility for the acts of his agents or representatives, it cannot legally or reasonably be said that anybody at all supports the Constitution by voting. No man can reasonably or legally be said to do such a thing as assent to, or support, the Constitution, UNLESS HE DOES IT OPENLY, AND IN A WAY TO MAKE HIMSELF PERSONALLY RESPONSIBLE FOR THE ACTS OF HIS AGENTS, SO LONG AS THEY ACT WITHIN THE LIMITS OF THE POWER HE DELEGATES TO THEM.

10. As all voting is secret (by secret ballot), and as all secret governments are necessarily only secret bands of robbers, tyrants, and murderers, the general fact that our government is practically carried on by means of such voting, only proves that there is among us a secret band of robbers, tyrants, and murderers, whose purpose is to rob, enslave, and, so far as necessary to accomplish their purposes, murder, the rest of the people. The simple fact of the existence of such a vand does nothing towards proving that "the people of the United States," or any one of them, voluntarily supports the Constitution.

For all the reasons that have now been given, voting furnishes no legal evidence as to who the particular individuals are (if there are any), who voluntarily support the Constitution. It therefore furnishes no legal evidence that anybody supports it voluntarily.

So far, therefore, as voting is concerned, the Constitution, legally speaking, has no supporters at all.

And, as a matter of fact, there is not the slightest probability that the Constitution has a single bona fide supporter in the country. That is to say, there is not the slightest probability that there is a single man in the country, who both understands what the Constitution really is, AND SINCERELY SUPPORTS IT FOR WHAT IT REALLY IS.

The ostensible supporters of the Constitution, like the ostensible supporters of most other governments, are made up of three classes, viz.: 1. Knaves, a numerous and active class, who see in the government an instrument which they can use for their own aggrandizement or wealth. 2. Dupes – a large class, no doubt – each of whom, because he is allowed one voice out of millions in deciding what he may do with his own person and his own property, and because he is permitted to have the same voice in robbing, enslaving, and murdering others, that others have in robbing, enslaving, and murdering himself, is stupid enough to imagine that he is a "free man," a "sovereign"; that this is "a free government"; "a government of equal rights," "the best government on earth," and such like absurdities. (Note: Suppose it be "the best government on earth," does that prove its own goodness, or only the badness of all other governments?) 3. A class who have some appreciation of the evils of government, but either do not see how to get rid of them, or do not choose to so far sacrifice their private interests as to give themselves seriously and earnestly to the work of making a change.

Chapter 3

The payment of taxes, being compulsory, of course furnishes no evidence that any one voluntarily supports the Constitution.

1. It is true that the THEORY of our Constitution is, that all taxes are paid voluntarily; that our government is a mutual insurance company, voluntarily entered into by the people with each other; that that each man makes a free and purely voluntary contract with all others who are parties to the Constitution, to pay so much money for so much protection, the same as he does with any other insurance company; and that he is just as free not to be protected, and not to pay tax, as he is to pay a tax, and be protected.

But this theory of our government is wholly different from the practical fact. The fact is that the government, like a highwayman, says to a man: "Your money, or your life." And many, if not most, taxes are paid under the compulsion of that threat.

The government does not, indeed, waylay a man in a lonely place, spring upon him from the roadside, and, holding a pistol to his head, proceed to rifle his pockets. But the robbery is none the less a robbery on that account; and it is far more dastardly and shameful.

The highwayman takes solely upon himself the responsibility, danger, and crime of his own act. He does not pretend that he has any rightful claim to your money, or that he intends to use it for your own benefit. He does not pretend to be anything but a robber. He has not acquired impudence enough to profess to be merely a "protector," and that he takes men's money against their will, merely to enable him to "protect" those infatuated travellers, who feel perfectly able to protect themselves, or do not appreciate his peculiar system of protection. He is too sensible a man to make such professions as these. Furthermore, having taken your money, he leaves you, as you wish him to do. He does not persist in following you on the road, against your will; assuming to be your rightful "sovereign," on account of the "protection" he affords you. He does not keep "protecting" you, by commanding you to bow down and serve him; by requiring you to do this, and forbidding you to do that; by robbing you of more money as often as he finds it for his interest or pleasure to do so; and by branding you as a rebel, a traitor, and an enemy to your country, and shooting you down without mercy, if you dispute his authority, or resist his demands. He is too much of a gentleman to be guilty of such impostures, and insults, and villanies as these. In short, he does not, in addition to robbing you, attempt to make you either his dupe or his slave.

The proceedings of those robbers and murderers, who call themselves "the government," are directly the opposite of these of the single highwayman.

In the first place, they do not, like him, make themselves individually known; or, consequently, take upon themselves personally the responsibility of their acts. On the contrary, they secretly (by secret ballot) designate some one of their number to commit the robbery in their behalf, while they keep themselves practically concealed. They say to the person thus designated:

Go to A_____ B_____, and say to him that "the government" has need of money to meet the expenses of protecting him and his property. If he presumes to say that he has never contracted with us to protect him, and that he wants none of our protection, say to him that that is our business, and not his; that we CHOOSE to protect him, whether he desires us to do so or not; and that we demand pay, too, for protecting him. If he dares to inquire who the individuals are, who have thus taken upon themselves the title of "the government," and who assume to protect him, and demand payment of him, without his having ever made any contract with them, say to him that that, too, is our business, and not his; that we do not CHOOSE to make ourselves INDIVIDUALLY known to him; that we have secretly (by secret ballot) appointed you our agent to give him notice of our demands, and, if he complies with them, to give him, in our name, a receipt that will protect him against any similar demand for the present year. If he refuses to comply, seize and sell enough of his property to pay not only our demands, but all your own expenses and trouble beside. If he resists the seizure of his property, call upon the bystanders to help you (doubtless some of them will prove to be members of our band.) If, in defending his property, he should kill any of our band who are assisting you, capture him at all hazards; charge him (in one of our courts) with murder; convict him, and hang him. If he should call upon his neighbors, or any others who, like him, may be disposed to resist our demands, and they should come in large numbers to his assistance, cry out that they are all rebels and traitors; that "our country" is in danger; call upon the commander of our hired murderers; tell him to quell the rebellion and "save the country," cost what it may. Tell him to kill all who resist, though they should be hundreds of thousands; and thus strike terror into all others similarly disposed. See that the work of murder is thoroughly done; that we may have no further trouble of this kind hereafter. When these traitors shall have thus been taught our strength and our determination, they will be good loyal citizens for many years, and pay their taxes without a why or a wherefore.

It is under such compulsion as this that taxes, so called, are paid. And how much proof the payment of taxes affords, that the people consent to "support the government," it needs no further argument to show.

2. Still another reason why the payment of taxes implies no consent, or pledge, to support the government, is that the taxpayer does not know, and has no means of knowing, who the particular individuals are who compose "the government." To him "the government" is a myth, an abstraction, an incorporeality, with which he can make no contract, and to which he can give no consent, and make no pledge. He knows it only through its pretended agents. "The government" itself he never sees. He knows indeed, by common report, that certain persons, of a certain age, are permitted to vote; and thus to make themselves parts of, or (if they choose) opponents of, the government, for the time being. But who of them do thus vote, and especially how each one votes (whether so as to aid or oppose the government), he does not know; the voting being all done secretly (by secret ballot). Who, therefore, practically compose "the government," for the time being, he has no means of knowing. Of course he can make no contract with them, give them no consent, and make them no pledge. Of necessity, therefore, his paying taxes to them implies, on his part, no contract, consent, or pledge to support

them – that is, to support "the government," or the Constitution.

3. Not knowing who the particular individuals are, who call themselves "the government," the taxpayer does not know whom he pays his taxes to. All he knows is that a man comes to him, representing himself to be the agent of "the government" – that is, the agent of a secret band of robbers and murderers, who have taken to themselves the title of "the government," and have determined to kill everybody who refuses to give them whatever money they demand. or save his life, he gives up his money to this agent. But as this agent does not make his principals individually known to the taxpayer, the latter, after he has given up his money, knows no more who are "the government" – that is, who were the robbers – than he did before. To say, therefore, that by giving up his money to their agent, he entered into a voluntary contract with them, that he pledges himself to obey them, to support them, and to give them whatever money they should demand of him in the future, is simply ridiculous.

4. All political power, so called, rests practically upon this matter of money. Any number of scoundrels, having money enough to start with, can establish themselves as a "government"; because, with money, they can hire soldiers, and with soldiers extort more money; and also compel general obedience to their will. It is with government, as Caesar said it was in war, that money and soldiers mutually supported each other; that with money he could hire soldiers, and with soldiers extort money. So these villains, who call themselves governments, well understand that their power rests primarily upon money. With money they can hire soldiers,

and with soldiers extort money. And, when their authority is denied, the first use they always make of money, is to hire soldiers to kill or subdue all who refuse them more money.

For this reason, whoever desires liberty, should understand these vital facts, viz.: 1. That every man who puts money into the hands of a "government" (so called), puts into its hands a sword which will be used against him, to extort more money from him, and also to keep him in subjection to its arbitrary will. 2. That those who will take his money, without his consent, in the first place, will use it for his further robbery and enslavement, if he presumes to resist their demands in the future. 3. That it is a perfect absurdity to suppose that any body of men would ever take a man's money without his consent, for any such object as they profess to take it for, viz., that of protecting him; for why should they wish to protect him, if he does not wish them to do so? To suppose that they would do so, is just as absurd as it would be to suppose that they would take his moeny without his consent, for the purpose of buying food or clothing for him, when he did not want it. 4. If a man wants "protection," he is competent to make his own bargains for it; and nobody has any occasion to rob him, in order to "protect" him against his will. 5. That the only security men can have for their political liberty, consists in their keeping their money in their own pockets, until they have assurances, perfectly satisfactory to themselves, that it will be used as they wish it to be used, for their benefit, and not for their injury. 6. That no government, so called, can reasonably be trusted for a moment, or reasonably be supposed to have honest purposes in view, any longer than it depends wholly upon voluntary support.

These facts are all so vital and so self-evident, that it cannot reasonably be supposed that any one will voluntarily pay money to a "government," for the purpose of securing its protection, unless he first make an explicit and purely voluntary contract with it for that purpose.

It is perfectly evident, therefore, that neither such voting, nor such payment of taxes, as actually takes place, proves anybody's consent, or obligation, to support the Constitution. Consequently we have no evidence at all that the Constitution is binding upon anybody, or that anybody is under any contract or obligation whatever to support it. And nobody is under any obligation to support it.

Chapter 4

"THE CONSTITUTION NOT ONLY BINDS NOBODY NOW, BUT IT NEVER DID BIND ANYBODY."

It never bound anybody, because it was never agreed to by anybody in such a manner as to make it, on general principles of law and reason, binding upon him.

It is a general principle of law and reason, that a WRITTEN instrument binds no one until he has signed it. This principle is so inflexible a one, that even though a man is unable to write his name, he must still "make his mark," before he is bound by a written contract. This custom was established ages ago, when few men could write their names; when a clerk - that is, a man who could write - was so rare and valuable a person, that even if he were guilty of high crimes, he was entitled to pardon, on the ground that the public could not afford to lose his services. Even at that time, a written contract must be signed; and men who could not write, either "made their mark," or signed their contracts by stamping their seals upon wax affixed to the parchment on which their contracts were written. Hence the custom of affixing seals, that has continued to this time.

The laws holds, and reason declares, that if a written instrument is not signed, the presumption must be that the party to be bound by it, did not choose to sign it, or to bind himself by it. And law and reason both give him until the last moment, in which to decide whether he will sign it, or not. Neither law nor reason requires or expects a man to agree to an instrument, UNTIL IT IS WRITTEN; for until it is written, he cannot know its precise legal meaning. And when it is written, and he has had the opportunity to satisfy himself of its precise legal meaning, he is then expected to decide, and not before, whether he will agree to it or not. And if he do not THEN sign it, his reason is supposed to be, that he does not choose to enter into such a contract. The fact that the instrument was written for him to sign, or with the hope that he would sign it, goes for nothing.

Where would be the end of fraud and litigation, if one party could bring into court a written instrument, without any signature, and claim to have it enforced, upon the ground that it was written for another man to sign? that this other man had promised to sign it? that he ought to have signed it? that he had had the opportunity to sign it, if he would? but that he had refused or neglected to do so? Yet that is the most that could ever be said of the Constitution. [1] The very judges, who profess to derive all their authority from the Constitution - from an instrument that nobody ever signed - would spurn any other instrument, not signed, that should be brought before them for adjudication.

[1] The very men who drafted it, never signed it in any way to bind themselves by it, AS A CONTRACT. And not one of them probably ever would have signed it in any way to bind himself by it, AS A CONTRACT.

Moreover, a written instrument must, in law and reason, not only be signed, but must also be delivered to the party (or to some one for him), in whose favor it is made, before it can bind the party making it. The signing is of no effect, unless the instrument be also delivered. And a party is at perfect liberty to refuse to deliver a written instrument, after he has signed it. The

Constitution was not only never signed by anybody, but it was never delivered by anybody, or to anybody's agent or attorney. It can therefore be of no more validity as a contract, then can any other instrument that was never signed or delivered.

Chapter 5

As further evidence of the general sense of mankind, as to the practical necessity there is that all men's IMPORTANT contracts, especially those of a permanent nature, should be both written and signed, the following facts are pertinent.

For nearly two hundred years - that is, since 1677 - there has been on the statute book of England, and the same, in substance, if not precisely in letter, has been re-enacted, and is now in force, in nearly or quite all the States of this Union, a statute, the general object of which is to declare that no action shall be brought to enforce contracts of the more important class, UNLESS THEY ARE PUT IN WRITING, AND SIGNED BY THE PARTIES TO BE HELD CHARGEABLE UPON THEM. [At this point there is a footnote listing 34 states whose statute books Spooner had examined, all of which had variations of this English statute; the footnote also quotes part of the Massachussetts statute.]

The principle of the statute, be it observed, is, not merely that written contracts shall be signed, but also that all contracts, except for those specially exempted - generally those that are for small amounts, and are to remain in force for but a short time - SHALL BE BOTH WRITTEN AND SIGNED.

The reason of the statute, on this point, is, that it is now so easy a thing for men to put their contracts in writing, and sign them, and their failure to do so opens the door to so much doubt, fraud, and litigation, that men who neglect to have their contracts - of any considerable importance - written and signed, ought not to have the benefit of courts of justice to enforce them. And this reason is a wise one; and that experience has confirmed its wisdom and necessity, is demonstrated by the fact that it has been acted upon in England for nearly two hundred years, and has been so nearly universally adopted in this country, and that nobody thinks of repealing it.

We all know, too, how careful most men are to have their contracts written and signed, even when this statute does not require it. For example, most men, if they have money due them, of no larger amount than five or ten dollars, are careful to take a note for it. If they buy even a small bill of goods, paying for it at the time of delivery, they take a receipted bill for it. If they pay a small balance of a book account, or any other small debt previously contracted, they take a written receipt for it.

Furthermore, the law everywhere (probably) in our country, as well as in England, requires that a large class of contracts, such as wills, deeds, etc., shall not only be written and signed, but also sealed, witnessed, and acknowledged. And in the case of married women conveying their rights in real estate, the law, in many States, requires that the women shall be examined separate and apart from their husbands, and declare that they sign their contracts free of any fear or compulsion of their husbands.

Such are some of the precautions which the laws require, and which individuals - from motives of common prudence, even in cases not required by law - take, to put their contracts in writing, and have them signed, and, to guard against all uncertainties and controversies in regard to their meaning and validity. And yet we have what purports, or professes, or is claimed, to be a contract - the Constitution - made eighty years ago, by men who are now all dead, and who never had any power to bind US, but which (it is claimed) has nevertheless bound three generations of men, consisting of many millions, and which (it is claimed) will be binding upon all the millions that are to come; but which nobody ever signed, sealed, delivered, witnessed, or acknowledged; and which few persons, compared with the whole number that are claimed to be bound by it, have ever read, or even seen, or ever will read, or see. And of those who ever have read it, or ever will read it, scarcely any two, perhaps no two, have ever agreed, or ever will agree, as to what it means.

Moreover, this supposed contract, which would not be received in any court of justice sitting under its authority, if offered to prove a debt of five dollars, owing by one man to another, is one by which - AS IT IS GENERALLY INTERPRETED BY THOSE WHO PRETEND TO ADMINISTER IT - all men, women and children throughout the country, and through all time, surrender not only all their property, but also their liberties, and even lives, into the hands of men who by this supposed contract, are expressly made wholly irresponsible for their disposal of them. And we are so insane, or so wicked, as to destroy property and lives without limit, in fighting to compel men to fulfill a supposed contract, which, inasmuch as it has never been signed by anybody, is, on general princples of law and reason - such principles as we are all governed by in regard to other contracts - the merest waste of paper, binding upon nobody, fit only to be thrown into the fire; or, if preserved, preserved only to serve as a witness and a warning of the folly and wickedness of mankind.

Chapter 6

It is no exaggeration, but a literal truth, to say that, by the Constitution - NOT AS I INTERPRET IT, BUT AS IT IS INTERPRETED BY THOSE WHO PRETEND TO ADMINISTER IT - the properties, liberties, and lives of the entire people of the United States are surrendered unreservedly into the hands of men who, it is provided by the Constitution itself, shall never be "questioned" as to any disposal they make of them.

Thus the Constitution (Art. I, Sec. 6) provides that, "for any speech or debate (or vote), in either house, they (the senators and representatives) shall not be questioned in any other place."

The whole lawmaking power is given to these senators and representatives (when acting by a two-thirds vote); [1] and this provision protects them from all responsibility for the laws they make.

[1] And this two-thirds vote may be but two-thirds of a quorum - that is two-thirds of a majority - instead of two-thirds of the whole.

The Constitution also enables them to secure the execution of all their laws, by giving them power to withhold the salaries of, and to impeach and remove, all judicial and executive officers, who refuse to execute them.

Thus the whole power of the government is in their hands, and they are made utterly irresponsible for the use they make of it. What is this but absolute, irresponsible power?

It is no answer to this view of the case to say that these men are under oath to use their power only within certain limits; for what care they, or what should they care, for oaths or limits, when it is expressly provided, by the Constitution itself, that they shall never be "questioned," or held to any resonsibility whatever, for violating their oaths, or transgressing those limits?

Neither is it any answer to this view of the case to say that the men holding this absolute, irresponsible power, must be men chosen by the people (or portions of them) to hold it. A man is none the less a slave because he is allowed to choose a new master once in a term of years. Neither are a people any the less slaves because permitted periodically to choose new masters. What makes them slaves is the fact that they now are, and are always hereafter to be, in the hands of men whose power over them is, and always is to be, absolute and irresponsible. (Note: Of what appreciable value is it to any man, as an individual, that he is allowed a voice in choosing these public masters? His voice is only one of several millions.)

The right of absolute and irresponsible dominion is the right of property, and the right of property is the right of absolute, irresponsible dominion. The two are identical; the one necessarily implies the other. Neither can exist without the other. If, therefore, Congress have that absolute and irresponsible lawmaking power, which the Constitution – according to their interpretation of it – gives them, it can only be because they own us as property. If they own us as property, they are our masters, and their will is our law. If they do not own us as property, they are not our masters, and their will, as such, is of no authority over us.

But these men who claim and exercise this absolute and irresponsible dominion over us, dare not be consistent, and claim either to be our masters, or to own us as property. They say they are only our servants, agents, attorneys, and representatives. But this declaration involves an absurdity, a contradiction. No man can be my servant, agent, attorney, or representative, and be, at the same time, uncontrollable by me, and irresponsible to me for his acts. It is of no importance that I appointed him, and put all power in his hands. If I made him uncontrollable by me, and irresponsible to me, he is no longer my servant, agent, attorney, or representative. If I gave him absolute, irresponsible power over my property, I gave him the property. If I gave him absolute, irresponsible power over myself, I made him my master, and gave myself to him as a slave. And it is of no importance whether I called him master or servant, agent or owner. The only question is, what power did I put in his hands? Was it an absolute and irresponsible one? or a limited and responsible one?

For still another reason they are neither our servants, agents, attorneys, nor representatives. And that reason is, that we do not make ourselves responsible for their acts. If a man is my servant, agent, or attorney, I necessarily make myself responsible for all his acts done within the limits of the power I have intrusted to him. If I have intrusted him, as my agent, with either absolute power, or any power at all, over the persons or properties of other men than myself, I thereby necessarily make myself responsible to those other persons for any injuries he may do them, so long as he acts within the limits of the power I have granted him. But no individual who may be injured in his person or property, by acts of Congress, can come to the individual electors, and hold them responsible for these acts of their so-called agents or representatives. This fact proves that these pretended agents of the people, of everybody, are really the agents of nobody.

If, then, nobody is individually responsible for the acts of Congress, the members of Congress are nobody's agents. And if they are nobody's agents, they are themselves individually responsible for their own acts, and for the acts of all whom they employ. And the authority they are exercising is simply their own individual authority; and, by the law of nature - the highest of all laws - anybody injured by their acts, anybody who is deprived by them of his property or his liberty, has the same right to hold them individually responsible, that he has to hold any other trespasser individually responsible. He has the same right to resist them, and their agents, that he has to resist any other trespassers.

Chapter 7

It is plain, then, that on general principles of law and reason - such principles as we all act upon in courts of justice and in common life - the Constitution is no contract; that it binds nobody, and never did bind anybody; and that all those who pretend to act by its authority, are really acting without any legitimate authority at all; that, on general principles of law and reason, they are mere usurpers, and that everybody not only has the right, but is morally bound, to treat them as such.

If the people of this country wish to maintain such a government as the Constitution describes, there is no reason in the world why they should not sign the instrument itself, and thus make known their wishes in an open, authentic manner; in such manner as the common sense and experience of mankind have shown to be reasonable and necessary in such cases; AND IN SUCH MANNER AS TO MAKE THEMSELVES (AS THEY OUGHT TO DO) INDIVIDUALLY RESPONSIBLE FOR THE ACTS OF THE GOVERNMENT. But the people have never been asked to sign it. And the only reason why they have never been asked to sign it, has been that it has been known that they never would sign it; that they were neither such fools nor knaves as they must needs have been to be willing to sign it; that (at least as it has been practically interpreted) it is not what any sensible and honest man wants for himself; nor such as he has any right to impose upon others. It is, to all moral intents and purposes, as destitute of obligations as the compacts which robbers and thieves and pirates enter into with each other, but never sign.

If any considerable number of the people believe the Constitution to be good, why do they not sign it themselves, and make laws for, and administer them upon, each other; leaving all other persons (who do not interfere with them) in peace? Until they have tried the experiment for themselves, how can they have the face to impose the Constitution upon, or even to recommend it to, others? Plainly the reason for absurd and inconsistent conduct is that they want the Constitution, not solely for any honest or legitimate use it can be of to themselves or others, but for the dishonest and illegitimate power it gives them over the persons and properties of others. But for this latter reason, all their eulogiums on the Constitution, all their exhortations, and all their expenditures of money and blood to sustain it, would be wanting.

Chapter 8

The Constitution itself, then, being of no authority, on what authority does our government practically rest? On what ground can those who pretend to administer it, claim the right to seize men's property, to restrain them of their natural liberty of action, industry, and trade, and to kill all who deny their authority to dispose of men's properties, liberties, and lives at their pleasure or discretion?

The most they can say, in answer to this question, is, that some half, two-thirds, or three-fourths, of the male adults of the country have a TACIT UNDERSTANDING that they will maintain a government under the Constitution; that they will select, by ballot, the persons to administer it; and that those persons who may receive a majority, or a plurality, of their ballots, shall act as their representatives, and administer the Constitution in their name, and by their authority.

But this tacit understanding (admitting it to exist) cannot at all justify the conclusion drawn from it. A tacit understanding between A, B, and C, that they will, by ballot, depute D as their agent, to deprive me of my property, liberty, or life, cannot at all authorize D to do so. He is none the less a robber, tyrant, and murderer, because he claims to act as their agent, than he would be if he avowedly acted on his own responsibility alone.

Neither am I bound to recognize him as their agent, nor can he legitimately claim to be their agent, when he brings no WRITTEN authority from them accrediting him as such. I am under no obligation to take his word as to who his principals may be, or whether he has any. Bringing no credentials, I have a right to say he has no such authority even as he claims to have: and that he is therefore intending to rob, enslave, or murder me on his own account.

This tacit understanding, therefore, among the voters of the country, amounts to nothing as an authority to their agents. Neither do the ballots by which they select their agents, avail any more than does their tacit understanding; for their ballots are given in secret, and therefore in such a way as to avoid any personal responsibility for the acts of their agents.

No body of men can be said to authorize a man to act as their agent, to the injury of a third person, unless they do it in so open and authentic a manner as to make themselves personally responsible for his acts. None of the voters in this country appoint their political agents in any open, authentic manner, or in any manner to make themselves responsible for their acts. Therefore these pretended agents cannot legitimately claim to be really agents. Somebody must be responsible for the acts of these pretended agents; and if they cannot show any open and authentic credentials from their principals, they cannot, in law or reason, be said to have any principals. The maxim applies here, that what does not appear, does not exist. If they can show no principals, they have none.

But even these pretended agents do not themselves know who their pretended principals are. These latter act in secret; for acting by secret ballot is acting in secret as much as if they were to meet in secret conclave in the darkness of the night. And they are personally as much unknown to the agents they select, as they are to others. No pretended agent therefore can ever know by whose ballots he is selected, or consequently who his real principles are. Not knowing who his principles are, he has no right to say that he has any. He can, at most, say only that he is the agent of a secret band of robbers and murderers, who are bound by that faith which prevails among confederates in crime, to stand by him, if his acts, done in their name, shall be resisted.

Men honestly engaged in attempting to establish justice in the world, have no occasion thus to act in secret; or to appoint agents to do acts for which they (the principals) are not willing to be responsible.

The secret ballot makes a secret government; and a secret government is a secret band of robbers and murderers. Open despotism is better than this. The single despot stands out in the face of all men, and says: I am the State: My will is law: I am your master: I take the responsibility of my acts: The only arbiter I acknowledge is the sword: If anyone denies my right, let him try conclusions with me.

But a secret government is little less than a government of assassins. Under it, a man knows not who his tyrants are, until they have struck, and perhaps not then. He may GUESS, beforehand, as to some of his immediate neighbors. But he really knows nothing. The man to whom he would most naturally fly for protection, may prove an enemy, when the time of trial comes.

This is the kind of government we have; and it is the only one we are likely to have, until men are ready to say: We will consent to no Constitution, except such an one as we are neither ashamed nor afraid to sign; and we will authorize no government to do anything in our name which we are not willing to be personally responsible for.

Chapter 9

What is the motive to the secret ballot? This, and only this: Like other confederates in crime, those who use it are not friends, but enemies; and they are afraid to be known, and to have their individual doings known, even to each other. They can contrive to bring about a sufficient understanding to enable them to act in concert against other persons; but beyond this they have no confidence, and no friendship, among themselves. In fact, they are engaged quite as much in schemes for plundering each other, as in plundering those who are not of them. And it is perfectly well understood among them that the strongest party among them will, in certain contingencies, murder each other by the hundreds of thousands (as they lately did do) to accomplish their purposes against each other. Hence they dare not be known, and have their individual doings known, even to each other. And this is avowedly the only reason for the ballot: for a secret government; a government by secret bands of robbers and murderers. And we are insane enough to call this liberty! To be a member of this secret band of robbers and murderers is esteemed a privilege and an honor! Without this privilege, a man is considered a slave; but with it a free man! With it he is considered a free man, because he has the same power to secretly (by secret ballot) procure the robbery, enslavement, and murder of another man, and that other man has to procure his robbery, enslavement, and murder. And this they call equal rights!

If any number of men, many or few, claim the right to govern the people of this country, let them make and sign an open compact with each other to do so. Let them thus make themselves individually known to those whom they propose to govern. And let them thus openly take the legitimate responsibility of their acts. How many of those who now support the Constitution, will ever do this? How many will ever dare openly proclaim their right to govern? or take the legitimate responsibility of their acts? Not one!

Chapter 10

It is obvious that, on general principles of law and reason, there exists no such thing as a government created by, or resting upon, any consent, compact, or agreement of "the people of the United States" with each other; that the only visible, tangible, responsible government that exists, is that of a few individuals only, who act in concert, and call themselves by the several names of senators, representatives, presidents, judges, marshals, treasurers, collectors, generals, colonels, captains, etc., etc.

On general principles of law and reason, it is of no importance whatever that these few individuals profess to be the agents and representatives of "the people of the United States"; since they can show no credentials from the people themselves; they were never appointed as agents or representatives in any open, authentic manner; they do not themselves know, and have no means of knowing, and cannot prove, who their principals (as they call them) are individually; and consequently cannot, in law or reason, be said to have any principals at all.

It is obvious, too, that if these alleged principals ever did appoint these pretended agents, or representatives, they appointed them secretly (by secret ballot), and in a way to avoid all personal responsibility for their acts; that, at most, these alleged principals put these pretended agents forward for the most criminal purposes, viz.: to plunder the people of their property, and restrain them of their liberty; and that the only authority that these alleged principals have for so doing, is simply a

TACIT UNDERSTANDING among themselves that they will imprison, shoot, or hang every man who resists the exactions and restraints which their agents or representatives may impose upon them.

Thus it is obvious that the only visible, tangible government we have is made up of these professed agents or representatives of a secret band of robbers and murderers, who, to cover up, or gloss over, their robberies and murders, have taken to themselves the title of "the people of the United States"; and who, on the pretense of being "the people of the United States," assert their right to subject to their dominion, and to control and dispose of at their pleasure, all property and persons found in the United States.

Chapter 11

On general principles of law and reason, the oaths which these pretended agents of the people take "to support the Constitution," are of no validity or obligation. And why? For this, if for no other reason, viz., THAT THEY ARE GIVEN TO NOBODY. There is no privity (as the lawyers say) - that is, no mutual recognition, consent, and agreement - between those who take these oaths, and any other persons.

If I go upon Boston Common, and in the presence of a hundred thousand people, men, women and children, with whom I have no contract upon the subject, take an oath that I will enforce upon them the laws of Moses, of Lycurgus, of Solon, of Justinian, or of Alfred, that oath is, on general principles of law and reason, of no obligation. It is of no obligation, not merely because it is intrinsically a criminal one, BUT ALSO BECAUSE IT IS GIVEN TO NOBODY, and consequently pledges my faith to nobody. It is merely given to the winds.

It would not alter the case at all to say that, among these hundred thousand persons, in whose presence the oath was taken, there were two, three, or five thousand male adults, who had SECRETLY - by secret ballot, and in a way to avoid making themselves INDIVIDUALLY known to me, or to the remainder of the hundred thousand - designated me as their agent to rule, control, plunder, and, if need be, murder, these hundred thousand people. The fact that they had designated me secretly, and in a manner to prevent my knowing them individually, prevents all privity between them and me; and consequently makes it impossible that there can be any contract, or pledge of faith, on my part towards them; for it is impossible that I can pledge my faith, in any legal sense, to a man whom I neither know, nor have any means of knowing, individually.

So far as I am concerned, then, these two, three, or five thousand persons are a secret band of robbers and murderers, who have secretly, and in a way to save themselves from all responsibility for my acts, designated me as their agent; and have, through some other agent, or pretended agent, made their wishes known to me. But being, nevertheless, individually unknown to me, and having no open, authentic contract with me, my oath is, on general principles of law and reason, of no validity as a pledge of faith to them. And being no pledge of faith to them, it is no pledge of faith to anybody. It is mere idle wind. At most, it is only a pledge of faith to an unknown band of robbers and murderers, whose instrument for plundering and murdering other people, I thus publicly confess myself to be. And it has no other obligation than a similar oath given to any other unknown body of pirates, robbers, and murderers.

For these reasons the oaths taken by members of Congress, "to support the Constitution," are, on general principles of law and reason, of no validity. They are not only criminal in themselves, and therefore void; but they are also void for the further reason THAT THEY ARE GIVEN TO NOBODY.

It cannot be said that, in any legitimate or legal sense, they are given to "the people of the United States"; because neither the whole, nor any large proportion of the whole, people of the United States ever, either openly or secretly, appointed or designated these men as their agents to carry the Constitution into effect. The great body of the people - that is, men, women, and children - were never asked, or even permitted, to signify, in any FORMAL manner, either openly or secretly, their choice or wish on the subject. The most that these members of Congress can say, in favor of their appointment, is simply this: Each one can say for himself:

I have evidence satisfactory to myself, that there exists, scattered throughout the country, a band of men, having a tacit understanding with each other, and calling themselves "the people of the United States," whose general purposes are to control and plunder each other, and all other persons in the country, and, so far as they can, even in neighboring countries; and to kill every man who shall attempt to defend his person and property against their schemes of plunder and dominion. Who these men are, INDIVIDUALLY, I have no certain means of knowing, for they sign no papers, and give no open, authentic evidence of their individual membership. They are not known individually even to each other. They are apparently as much afraid of being individually known to each other, as of being known to other persons. Hence they ordinarily have no mode either of exercising, or of making known, their individual membership, otherwise than by giving their votes secretly for certain agents to do their will. \ But although these men are individually unknown, both to each other and to other persons, it is generally understood in the country that none but male persons, of the age of twenty-one years and upwards, can be members. It is also generally understood that ALL male persons, born in the country, having certain complexions, and (in some localities) certain amounts of property, and (in certain cases) even persons of foreign birth, are PERMITTED to be members. But it appears that usually not more than one half, two-thirds, or in some cases, three-fourths, of all who are thus permitted to become members of the band, ever exercise, or consequently prove, their actual membership, in the only mode in which they ordinarily can exercise or prove it, viz., by giving their votes secretly for the officers or agents of the band. The number of these secret votes, so far as we have any account of them, varies greatly from year to year, thus tending to prove that the band, instead of being a permanent organization, is a merely PRO TEMPORE affair with those who choose to act with it for the time being. \ The gross number of these secret votes, or what purports to be their gross number, in different localities, is occasionally published. Whether these reports are accurate or not, we have no means of knowing. It is generally supposed that great frauds are often committed in depositing them. They are understood to be received and counted by certain men, who are themselves appointed for that purpose by the same secret process by which all other officers and agents of the band are selected. According to the reports of these receivers of votes (for whose accuracy or honesty, however, I cannot vouch), and according to my best knowledge of the whole number of male persons "in my district," who (it is supposed) were permitted to vote, it would appear that one-half, two-thirds or three-fourths actually did vote. Who the men were, individually, who cast these votes, I have no knowledge, for the whole thing was done secretly. But of the secret votes thus given for what they call a "member of Congress," the receivers reported that I had a majority, or at least a larger number than any other one person. And it is only by virtue of such a designation that I am now here to act in concert with other persons similarly selected in other parts of the country. It is understood among those who sent me here, that all persons so selected, will, on coming together at the City of Washington, take an oath in each other's presence "to support the Constitution of the United States." By this is meant a certain paper that was drawn up eighty years ago. It was never signed by anybody, and apparently has no obligation, and never had any obligation, as a contract. In fact, few persons ever read it, and doubtless much the largest number of those who voted for me and the others, never even saw it, or now pretend to know what it means. Nevertheless, it is often spoken of in the country as "the Constitution of the United States"; and for some reason or other, the men who sent me here, seem to expect that I, and all with whom I act, will swear to carry this Constitution into effect. I am therefore ready to take this oath, and to co-operate with all others, similarly selected, who are ready to take the same oath.

This is the most that any member of Congress can say in proof that he has any constituency; that he represents anybody; that his oath "to support the Constitution," IS GIVEN TO ANYBODY, or pledges his faith to ANYBODY. He has no open, written, or other authentic evidence, such as is required in all other cases, that he was ever appointed the agent or representative of anybody. He has no written power of attorney from any single individual. He has no such legal knowledge as is required in all other cases, by which he can identify a single one of those who pretend to have appointed him to represent them.

Of course his oath, professedly given to them, "to support the Constitution," is, on general principles of law and reason, an oath given to nobody. It pledges his faith to nobody. If he fails to fulfil his oath, not a single person can come forward, and say to him, you have betrayed me, or broken faith with me.

No one can come forward and say to him: I appointed you my attorney to act for me. I required you to swear that, as my attorney, you would support the Constitution. You promised me that you would do so; and now you have forfeited the oath you gave to me. No single individual can say this.

No open, avowed, or responsible association, or body of men, can come forward and say to him: We appointed you our attorney, to act forus. We required you to swear that, as our attorney, you would support the Constitution. You promised us that you would do so; and now you have forfeited the oath you gave to us.

No open, avowed, or responsible association, or body of men, can say this to him; because there is no such association or body of men in existence. If any one should assert that there is such an association, let him prove, if he can, who compose it. Let him produce, if he can, any open, written, or other authentic contract, signed or agreed to by these men; forming themselves into an association; making themselves known as such to the world; appointing him as their agent; and making themselves individually, or as an association, responsible for his acts, done by their authority. Until all this can be shown, no one can say that, in any legitimate sense, there is any such association; or that he is their agent; or that he ever gave his oath to them; or ever pledged his faith to them.

On general principles of law and reason, it would be a sufficient answer for him to say, to all individuals, and to all pretended associations of individuals, who should accuse him of a breach of faith to them:

I never knew you. Where is your evidence that you, either individually or collectively, ever appointed me your attorney? that you ever required me to swear to you, that, as your attorney, I would support the Constitution? or that I have now broken any faith that I ever pledged to you? You may, or you may not, be members of that secret band of robbers and murderers, who act in secret; appoint their agents by a secret ballot; who keep themselves individually unknown even to the agents they thus appoint; and who, therefore, cannot claim that they have any agents; or that any of their pretended agents ever gave his oath, or pledged his faith to them. I repudiate you altogether. My oath was given to others, with whom you have nothing to do; or it was idle wind, given only to the idle winds. Begone!

Chapter 12

For the same reasons, the oaths of all the other pretended agents of this secret band of robbers and murderers are, on general principles of law and reason, equally destitute of obligation. They are given to nobody; but only to the winds.

The oaths of the tax-gatherers and treasurers of the band, are, on general principles of law and reason, of no validity. If any tax gatherer, for example, should put the money he receives into his own pocket, and refuse to part with it, the members of this band could not say to him: You collected that money as our agent, and for our uses; and you swore to pay it over to us, or to those we should appoint to receive it. You have betrayed us, and broken faith with us.

It would be a sufficient answer for him to say to them:

I never knew you. You never made yourselves individually known to me. I never game by oath to you, as individuals. You may, or you may not, be members of that secret band, who appoint agents to rob and murder other people; but who are cautious not to make themselves individually known, either to such agents, or to those whom their agents are commissioned to rob. If you are members of that band, you have given me no proof that you ever commissioned me to rob others for your benefit. I never knew you, as individuals, and of course never promised you that I would pay over to you the proceeds of my robberies. I committed my robberies on my own account, and for my own profit. If you thought I was fool enough to allow you to keep yourselves concealed, and use me as your tool for robbing other persons; or that I would take all the personal risk of the robberies, and pay over the proceeds to you, you were particularly simple. As I took all the risk of my robberies, I propose to take all the profits. Begone! You are fools, as well as villains. If I gave my oath to anybody, I gave it to other persons than you. But I really gave it to nobody. I only gave it to the winds. It answered my purposes at the time. It enabled me to get the money I was after, and now I propose to keep it. If you expected me to pay it over to you, you relied only upon that honor that is said to prevail among thieves. You now understand that that is a very poor reliance. I trust you may become wise enough to never rely upon it again. If I have any duty in the matter, it is to give back the money to those from whom I took it; not to pay it over to villains such as you.

Chapter 13

On general principles of law and reason, the oaths which foreigners take, on coming here, and being "naturalized" (as it is called), are of no validity. They are necessarily given to nobody; because there is no open, authentic association, to which they can join themselves; or to whom, as individuals, they can pledge their faith. No such association, or organization, as "the people of the United States," having ever been formed by any open, written, authentic, or voluntary contract, there is, on general principles of law and reason, no such association, or organization, in existence. And all oaths that purport to be given to such an association are necessarily given only to the winds. They cannot be said to be given to any man, or body of men, as individuals, because no man, or body of men, can come forward WITH ANY PROOF that the oaths were given to them, as individuals, or to any association of which they are members. To say that there is a tacit understanding among a portion of the male adults of the country, that they will call themselves "the people of the United States," and that they will act in concert in subjecting the remainder of the people of the United States to their dominion; but that they will keep themselves personally concealed by doing all their acts secretly, is wholly insufficient, on general principles of law and reason, to prove the existence of any such association, or organization, as "the people of the United States"; or consequently to prove that the oaths of foreigners were given to any such association.

Chapter 14

On general principles of law and reason, all the oaths which, since the war, have been given by Southern men, that they will obey the laws of Congress, support the Union, and the like, are of no validity. Such oaths are invalid, not only because they were extorted by military power, and threats of confiscation, and because they are in contravention of men's natural right to do as they please about supporting the government, BUT ALSO BECAUSE THEY WERE GIVEN TO NOBODY. They were nominally given to "the United States." But being nominally given to "the United States," they were necessarily given to nobody, because, on general principles of law and reason, there were no "United States," to whom the oaths could be given. That is to say, there was no open, authentic, avowed, legitimate association, corporation, or body of men, known as "the United States," or as "the people of the United States," to whom the oaths could have been given. If anybody says there was such a corporation, let him state who were the individuals that composed it, and how and when they became a corporation. Were Mr. A, Mr. B, and Mr. C members of it? If so, where are their signatures? Where the evidence of their membership? Where the record? Where the open, authentic proof? There is none. Therefore, in law and reason, there was no such corporation.

On general principles of law and reason, every corporation, association, or organized body of men, having a legitimate corporate existence, and legitimate corporate rights, must consist of certain known individuals, who can prove, by legitimate and reasonable evidence, their membership. But nothing of this kind can be proved in regard to the corporation, or body of men, who call themselves "the United States." Not a man of them, in all the Northern States, can prove by any legitimate evidence, such as is required to prove membership in other legal corporations, that he himself, or any other man whom he can name, is a member of any corporation or association called "the United States," or "the people of the United States," or, consequently, that there is any such corporation. And since no such corporation can be proved to exist, it cannot of course be proved that the oaths of Southern men were given to any such corporation. The most that can be claimed is that the oaths were given to a secret band of robbers and murderers, who called themselves "the United States," and extorted those oaths. But that is certainly not enough to prove that the oaths are of any obligation.

Chapter 15

On general principles of law and reason, the oaths of soldiers, that they will serve a given number of years, that they will obey the the orders of their superior officers, that they will bear true allegiance to the government, and so forth, are of no obligation. Independently of the criminality of an oath, that, for a given number of years, he will kill all whom he may be commanded to kill, without exercising his own judgment or conscience as to the justice or necessity of such killing, there is this further reason why a soldier's oath is of no obligation, viz., that, like all the other oaths that have now been mentioned, IT IS GIVEN TO NOBODY. There being, in no legitimate sense, any such corporation, or nation, as "the United States," nor, consequently, in any legitimate sense, any such government as "the government of the United States," a soldier's oath given to, or contract made with, such a nation or government, is necessarily an oath given to, or contract made with, nobody. Consequently such an oath or contract can be of no obligation.

Chapter 16

On general principles of law and reason, the treaties, so called, which purport to be entered into with other nations, by persons calling themselves ambassadors, secretaries, presidents, and senators of the United States, in the name, and in behalf, of "the people of the United States," are of no validity. These so-called ambassadors, secretaries, presidents, and senators, who claim to be the agents of "the people of the United States" for making these treaties, can show no open, written, or other authentic evidence that either the whole "people of the United States," or any other open, avowed, responsible body of men, calling themselves by that name, ever authorized these pretended ambassadors and others to make treaties in the name of, or binding upon any one of, "the people of the United States," or any other open, avowed, responsible body of men, calling themselves by that name, ever authorized these pretended ambassadors, secretaries, and others, in their name and behalf, to recognize certain other persons, calling themselves emperors, kings, queens, and the like, as the rightful rulers, sovereigns, masters, or representatives of the different peoples whom they assume to govern, to represent, and to bind.

The "nations," as they are called, with whom our pretended ambassadors, secretaries, presidents, and senators profess to make treaties, are as much myths as our own. On general principles of law and reason, there are no such "nations." That is to say, neither the whole people of England, for example, nor any open, avowed, responsible body of men, calling themselves by that name, ever, by any open, written, or other authentic contract with each other, formed themselves into any bona fide, legitimate association or organization, or authorized any king, queen, or other representative to make treaties in their name, or to bind them, either individually, or as an association, by such treaties.

Our pretended treaties, then, being made with no legitimate or bona fide nations, or representatives of nations, and being made, on our part, by persons who have no legitimate authority to act for us, have instrinsically no more validity than a pretended treaty made by the Man in the Moon with the king of the Pleiades.

Chapter 17

On general principles of law and reason, debts contracted in the name of "the United States," or of "the people of the United States," are of no validity. It is utterly absurd to pretend that debts to the amount of twenty-five hundred millions of dollars are binding upon thirty-five or forty millions of people [the approximate national debt and population in 1870], when there is not a particle of legitimate evidence – such as would be required to prove a private debt – that can be produced against any one of them, that either he, or his properly authorized attorney, ever contracted to pay one cent.

Certainly, neither the whole people of the United States, nor any number of them, ever separately or individually contracted to pay a cent of these debts.

Certainly, also, neither the whole people of the United States, nor any number of them, every, by any open, written, or other authentic and voluntary contract, united themselves as a firm, corporation, or association, by the name of "the United States," or "the people of the United States," and authorized their agents to contract debts in their name.

Certainly, too, there is in existence no such firm, corporation, or association as "the United States," or "the people of the United States," formed by any open, written, or other authentic and voluntary contract, and having corporate property with which to pay these debts.

How, then, is it possible, on any general principle of law or reason, that debts that are binding upon nobody individually, can be binding upon forty millions of people collectively, when, on general and legitimate principles of law and reason, these forty millions of people neither have, nor ever had, any corporate property? never made any corporate or individual contract? and neither have, nor ever had, any corporate existence?

Who, then, created these debts, in the name of "the United States"? Why, at most, only a few persons, calling themselves "members of Congress," etc., who pretended to represent "the people of the United States," but who really represented only a secret band of robbers and murderers, who wanted money to carry on the robberies and murders in which they were then engaged; and who intended to extort from the future people of the United States, by robbery and threats of murder (and real murder, if that should prove necessary), the means to pay these debts.

This band of robbers and murderers, who were the real principals in contracting these debts, is a secret one, because its members have never entered into any open, written, avowed, or authentic contract, by which they may be individually known to the world, or even to each other. Their real or pretended representatives, who contracted these debts in their name, were selected (if selected at all) for that purpose secretly (by secret ballot), and in a way to furnish evidence against none of the principals INDIVIDUALLY; and these principals were really known INDIVIDUALLY neither to their pretended representatives who contracted these debts in their behalf, nor to those who lent the money. The money, therefore, was all borrowed and lent in the dark; that is, by men who did not see each other's faces, or know each other's names; who could not then, and cannot now, identify each other as principals in the transactions; and who consequently can prove no contract with each other.

Furthermore, the money was all lent and borrowed for criminal purposes; that is, for purposes of robbery and murder; and for this reason the contracts were all intrinsically void; and would have been so, even though the real parties, borrowers and lenders, had come face to face, and made their contracts openly, in their own proper names.

Furthermore, this secret band of robbers and murderers, who were the real borrowers of this money, having no legitimate corporate existence, have no corporate property with which to pay these debts. They do indeed pretend to own large tracts of wild lands, lying between the Atlantic and Pacific Oceans, and between the Gulf of Mexico and the North Pole. But, on general principles of law and reason, they might as well pretend to own the Atlantic and Pacific Oceans themselves; or the atmosphere and the sunlight; and to hold them, and dispose of them, for the payment of these debts.

Having no corporate property with which to pay what purports to be their corporate debts, this secret band of robbers and murderers are really bankrupt. They have nothing to pay with. In fact, they do not propose to pay their debts otherwise than from the proceeds of their future robberies and murders. These are confessedly their sole reliance; and were known to be such by the lenders of the money, at the time the money was lent. And it was, therefore, virtually a part of the contract, that the money should be repaid only from the proceeds of these future robberies and murders. For this reason, if for no other, the contracts were void from the beginning.

In fact, these apparently two classes, borrowers and lenders, were really one and the same class. They borrowed and lent money from and to themselves. They themselves were not only part and parcel, but the very life and soul, of this secret band of robbers and murderers, who borrowed and spent the money. Individually they furnished money for a common enterprise; taking, in return, what purported to be corporate promises for individual loans. The only excuse they had for taking these so-called corporate promises of, for individual loans by, the same parties, was that they might have some apparent excuse for the future robberies of the band (that is, to pay the debts of the corporation), and that they might also know what shares they were to be respectively entitled to out of the proceeds of their future robberies.

Finally, if these debts had been created for the most innocent and honest purposes, and in the most open and honest manner, by the real parties to the contracts, these parties could thereby have bound nobody but themselves, and no property but their own. They could have bound nobody that should have come after them, and no property subsequently created by, or belonging to, other persons.

Chapter 18

The Constitution having never been signed by anybody; and there being no other open, written, or authentic contract between any parties whatever, by virtue of which the United States government, so called, is maintained; and it being well known that none but male persons, of twenty-one years of age and upwards, are allowed any voice in the government; and it being also well known that a large number of these adult persons seldom or never vote at all; and that all those who do vote, do so secretly (by secret ballot), and in a way to prevent their individual votes being known, either to the world, or even to each other; and consequently in a way to make no one openly responsible for the acts of their agents, or representatives, - all these things being known, the questions arise: WHO compose the real governing power in the country? Who are the men, THE RESPONSIBLE MEN, who rob us of our property? Restrain us of our liberty? Subject us to their arbitrary dominion? And devastate our hooms, and shoot us down by the hundreds of thousands, if we resist? How shall we find these men? How shall we know them from others? How shall we defend ourselves and our property against them? Who, of our neighbors, are members of this secret band of robbers and murderers? How can we know which are THEIR houses, that we may burn or demolish them? Which THEIR property, that we may destroy it? Which their persons, that we may kill them, and rid the world and ourselves of such tyrants and monsters?

These are questions that must be answered, before men can be free; before they can protect themselves against this secret band of robbers and murderers, who now plunder, enslave, and destroy them.

The answer to these questions is, that only those who have the will and power to shoot down their fellow men, are the real rulers in this, as in all other (so-called) civilized countries; for by no others will civilized men be robbed, or enslaved.

Among savages, mere physical strength, on the part of one man, may enable him to rob, enslave, or kill another man. Among barbarians, mere physical strength, on the part of a body of men, disciplined, and acting in concert, though with very little money or other wealth, may, under some circumstances, enable them to rob, enslave, or kill another body of men, as numerous, or perhaps even more numerous, than themselves. And among both savages and barbarians, mere want may sometimes compel one man to sell himself as a slave to another. But with (so-called) civilized peoples, among whom knowledge, wealth, and the means of acting in concert, have becom diffusede; and who have invented such weapons and other means of defense as to render mere physical strength of less importance; and by whom soldiers in any requisite number, and other instrumentalities of war in any requisite amount, can always be had for money, the question of war, and consequently the question of power, is little else than a mere question of money. As a necessary consequence, those who stand ready to furnish this money, are the real rulers. It is so in Europe, and it is so in this country.

In Europe, the nominal rulers, the emperors and kings and parliaments, are anything but the real rulers of their respective countries. They are little or nothing else than mere tools, employed by the wealthy to rob, enslave, and (if need be) murder those who have less wealth, or none at all.

The Rosthchilds, and that class of moneylenders of whom they are the representatives and agents - men who never think of lending a shilling to their next-door neighbors, for purposes of honest industry, unless upon the most ample security, and at the highest rate of interest - stand ready, at all times, to lend money in unlimited amounts to those robbers and murderers, who call themselves governments, to be expended in shooting down those who do not submit quietly to being robbed and enslaved.

They lend their money in this manner, knowing that it is to be expended in murdering their fellow men, for simply seeking their liberty and their rights; knowing also that neither the interest nor the principal will ever be paid, except as it will be extorted under terror of the repetition of such murders as those for which the money lent is to be expended.

These moneylenders, the Rosthchilds, for example, say to themselves: If we lend a hundred millions sterling to the queen and parliament of England, it will enable them to murder twenty, fifty, or a hundred thousand people in England, Ireland, or India; and the terror inspired by such wholesale slaughter, will enable them to keep the whole people of those countries in subjection for twenty, or perhaps fifty, years to come; to control all their trade and industry; and to extort from them large amounts of money, under the name of taxes; and from the wealth thus extorted from them, they (the queen and parliament) can afford to pay us a higher rate of interest for our money than we can get in any other way. Or, if we lend this sum to the emperor of Austria, it will enable him to murder so many of his people as to strike terror into the rest, and thus enable him to keep them in subjection, and extort money from them, for twenty or fifty years to come. And they say the same in regard to the emperor of Russia, the king of Prussia, the emperor of France, or any other ruler, so called, who, in their judgment, will be able, by murdering a reasonable portion of his people, to keep the rest in subjection, and extort money from them, for a long time to come, to pay the interest and the principal of the money lent him.

And why are these men so ready to lend money for murdering their fellow men? Soley for this reason, viz., that such loans are considered better investments than loans for purposes of honest industry. They pay higher rates of interest; and it is less trouble to look after them. This is the whole matter.

The question of making these loans is, with these lenders, a mere question of pecuniary profit. They lend money to be expended in robbing, enslaving, and murdering their fellow men, solely because, on the whole, such loans pay better than any others. They are no respecters of persons, no superstitious fools, that reverence monarchs. They care no more for a king, or an emperor, than they do for a beggar, except as he is a better customer, and can pay them better interest for their money. If they doubt his ability to make his murders successful for maintaining his power, and thus extorting money from his people in future, they dismiss him unceremoniously as they would dismiss any other hopeless bankrupt, who should want to borrow money to save himself from open insolvency.

When these great lenders of blood-money, like the Rothschilds, have loaned vast sums in this way, for purposes of murder, to an emperor or a king, they sell out the bonds taken by them, in small amounts, to anybody, and everybody, who are disposed to buy them at satisfactory prices, to hold as investments. They (the Rothschilds) thus soon get back their money, with great profits; and are now ready to lend money in the same way again to any other robber and murderer, called an emperor or king, who, they think, is likely to be successful in his robberies and murders, and able to pay a good price for the money necessary to carry them on.

This business of lending blood-money is one of the most thoroughly sordid, cold-blooded, and criminal that was ever carried on, to any considerable extent, amongst human beings. It is like lending money to slave traders, or to common robbers and pirates, to be repaid out of their plunder. And the men who loan money to governments, so called, for the purpose of enabling the latter to rob, enslave, and murder their people, are among the greatest villains that the world has ever seen. And they as much deserve to be hunted and killed (if they cannot otherwise be got rid of) as any slave traders, robbers, or pirates that ever lived.

When these emperors and kings, so-called, have obtained their loans, they proceed to hire and train immense numbers of professional murderers, called soldiers, and employ them in shooting down all who resist their demands for money. In fact, most of them keep large bodies of these murderers constantly in their service, as their only means of enforcing their extortions. There are now [1870], I think, four or five millions of these professional murderers constantly employed by the so-called sovereigns of Europe. The enslaved people are, of course, forced to support and pay all these murderers, as well as to submit to all the other extortions which these murderers are employed to enforce.

It is only in this way that most of the so-called governments of Europe are maintained. These so-called governments are in reality only great bands of robbers and murderers, organized, disciplined, and constantly on the alert. And the so-called sovereigns, in these different governments, are simply the heads, or chiefs, of different bands of robbers and murderers. And these heads or chiefs are dependent upon the lenders of blood-money for the means to carry on their robberies and murders. They could not sustain themselves a moment but for the loans made to them by these blood-money loan-mongers. And their first care is to maintain their credit with them; for they know their end is come, the instant their credit with them fails. Consequently the first proceeds of their extortions are scrupulously applied to the payment of the interest on their loans.

In addition to paying the interest on their bonds, they perhaps grant to the holders of them great monopolies in banking, like the Banks of England, of France, and of Vienna; with the agreement that these banks shall furnish money whenever, in sudden emergencies, it may be necessary to shoot down more of their people. Perhaps also, by means of tariffs on competing imports, they give great monopolies to certain branches of industry, in which these lenders of blood-money are engaged. They also, by unequal taxation, exempt wholly or partially the property of these loan-mongers, and throw corresponding burdens upon those who are too poor and weak to resist.

Thus it is evident that all these men, who call themselves by the high-sounding names of Emperors, Kings, Sovereigns, Monarchs, Most Christian Majesties, Most Catholic Majesties, High Mightinesses, Most Serene and Potent Princes, and the like, and who claim to rule "by the grace of God," by "Divine Right" – that is, by special authority from Heaven – are intrinsically not only the merest miscreants and wretches, engaged solely in plundering, enslaving, and murdering their fellow men, but that they are also the merest hangers on, the servile, obsequious, fawning dependents and tools of these blood-money loan-mongers, on whom they rely for the means to carry on their crimes. These loan-mongers, like the Rothschilds, laugh in their sleeves, and say to themselves: These despicable creatures, who call themselves emperors, and kings, and majesties, and most serene and potent princes; who profess to wear crowns, and sit on thrones; who deck themselves with ribbons, and feathers, and jewels; and surround themselves with hired flatterers and lickspittles; and whom we suffer to strut around, and palm themselves off, upon fools and slaves, as sovereigns and lawgivers specially appointed by Almighty God; and to hold themselves out as the sole fountains of honors, and dignities, and wealth, and power – all these miscreants and imposters know that we make them, and use them; that in us they live, move, and have their being; that we require them (as the price of their positions) to take upon themselves all the labor, all the danger, and all the odium of all the crimes they commit for our profit; and that we will unmake them, strip them of their gewgaws, and send them out into the world as beggars, or give them over to the vengeance of the people they have enslaved, the moment they refuse to commit any crime we require of them, or to pay over to us such share of the proceeds of their robberies as we see fit to demand.

Chapter 19

Now, what is true in Europe, is substantially true in this country. The difference is the immaterial one, that, in this country, there is no visible, permanent head, or chief, of these robbers and murderers who call themselves "the government." That is to say, there is no ONE MAN, who calls himself the state, or even emperor, king, or sovereign; no one who claims that he and his children rule "by the Grace of God," by "Divine Right," or by special appointment from Heaven. There are only certain men, who call themselves presidents, senators, and representatives, and claim to be the authorized agents, FOR THE TIME BEING, OR FOR CERTAIN SHORT PERIODS, OF ALL "the people of the United States"; but who can show no credentials, or powers of attorney, or any other open, authentic evidence that they are so; and who notoriously are not so; but are really only the agents of a secret band of robbers and murderers, whom they themselves do not know, and have no means of knowing, individually; but who, they trust, will openly or secretly, when the crisis comes, sustain them in all their usurpations and crimes.

What is important to be noticed is, that these so-called presidents, senators, and representatives, these pretended agents of all "the people of the United States," the moment their exactions meet with any formidable resistance from any portion of "the people" themselves, are obliged, like their co-robbers and murderers in Europe, to fly at once to the lenders of blood money, for the means to sustain their power. And they borrow their money on the same principle, and for the same purpose, viz., to be expended in shooting down all those "people of the United States" - their own constituents and principals, as they profess to call them - who resist the robberies and enslavements which these borrowers of the money are practising upon them. And they expect to repay the loans, if at all, only from the proceeds of the future robberies, which they anticipate it will be easy for them and their successors to perpetrate through a long series of years, upon their pretended principals, if they can but shoot down now some hundreds of thousands of them, and thus strike terror into the rest.

Perhaps the facts were never made more evident, in any country on the globe, than in our own, that these soulless blood-money loan-mongers are the real rulers; that they rule from the most sordid and mercenary motives; that the ostensible government, the presidents, senators, and representatives, so called, are merely their tools; and that no ideas of, or regard for, justice or liberty had anything to do in inducing them to lend their money for the war [i.e, the Civil War]. In proof of all this, look at the following facts.

Nearly a hundred years ago we professed to have got rid of all that religious superstition, inculcated by a servile and corrupt priesthood in Europe, that rulers, so called, derived their authority directly from Heaven; and that it was consequently a religious duty on the part of the people to obey them. We professed long ago to have learned that governments could rightfully exist only by the free will, and on the voluntary support, of those who might choose to sustain them. We all professed to have known long ago, that the only legitimate objects of government were the maintenance of liberty and justice equally for all. All this we had professed for nearly a hundred years. And we professed to look with pity and contempt upon those ignorant, superstitious, and enslaved peoples of Europe, who were so easily kept in subjection by the frauds and force of priests and kings.

Notwithstanding all this, that we had learned, and known, and professed, for nearly a century, these lenders of blood money had, for a long series of years previous to the war, been the willing accomplices of the slaveholders in perverting the government from the purposes of liberty and justice, to the greatest of crimes. They had been such accomplices FOR A PURELY PECUNIARY CONSIDERATION, to wit, a control of the markets in the South; in other words, the privilege of holding the slaveholders themselves in industrial and commercial subjection to the manufacturers and merchants of the North (who afterwards furnished the money for the war). And these Northern merchants and manufacturers, these lenders of blood-money, were willing to continue to be the accomplices of the slaveholders in the future, for the same pecuniary considerations. But the slaveholders, either doubting the fidelity of their Northern allies, or feeling themselves strong enough to keep their slaves in subjection without Northern assistance, would no longer pay the price which these Northern men demanded. And it was to enforce this price in the future - that is, to monopolize the Southern markets, to maintain their industrial and commercial control over the South - that these Northern manufacturers and merchants lent some of the profits of their former monopolies for the war, in order to secure to themselves the same, or greater, monopolies in the future. These - and not any love of liberty or justice - were the motives on which the money for the war was lent by the North. In short, the

North said to the slaveholders: If you will not pay us our price (give us control of your markets) for our assistance against your slaves, we will secure the same price (keep control of your markets) by helping your slaves against you, and using them as our tools for maintaining dominion over you; for the control of your markets we will have, whether the tools we use for that purpose be black or white, and be the cost, in blood and money, what it may.

On this principle, and from this motive, and not from any love of liberty, or justice, the money was lent in enormous amounts, and at enormous rates of interest. And it was only by means of these loans that the objects of the war were accomplished.

And now these lenders of blood-money demand their pay; and the government, so called, becomes their tool, their servile, slavish, villanous tool, to extort it from the labor of the enslaved people both of the North and South. It is to be extorted by every form of direct, and indirect, and unequal taxation. Not only the nominal debt and interest - enormous as the latter was - are to be paid in full; but these holders of the debt are to be paid still further - and perhaps doubly, triply, or quadruply paid - by such tariffs on imports as will enable our home manufacturers to realize enormous prices for their commodities; also by such monopolies in banking as will enable them to keep control of, and thus enslave and plunder, the industry and trade of the great body of the Northern people themselves. In short, the industrial and commercial slavery of the great body of the people, North and South, black and white, is the price which these lenders of blood money demand, and insist upon, and are determined to secure, in return for the money lent for the war.

This programme having been fully arranged and systematized, they put their sword into the hands of the chief murderer of the war, [undoubtedly a reference to General Grant, who had just become president] and charge him to carry their scheme into effect. And now he, speaking as their organ, says, "LET US HAVE PEACE."

The meaning of this is: Submit quietly to all the robbery and slavery we have arranged for you, and you can have "peace." But in case you resist, the same lenders of blood-money, who furnished the means to subdue the South, will furnish the means again to subdue you.

These are the terms on which alone this government, or, with few exceptions, any other, ever gives "peace" to its people.

The whole affair, on the part of those who furnished the money, has been, and now is, a deliberate scheme of robbery and murder; not merely to monopolize the markets of the South, but also to monopolize the currency, and thus control the industry and trade, and thus plunder and enslave the laborers, of both North and South. And Congress and the president are today the merest tools for these purposes. They are obliged to be, for they know that their own power, as rulers, so-called, is at an end, the moment their credit with the blood-money loan-mongers fails. They are like a bankrupt in the hands of an extortioner. They dare not say nay to any demand made upon them. And to hide at once, if possible, both their servility and crimes, they attempt to divert public attention, by crying out that they have

"Abolished Slavery!" That they have "Saved the Country!" That they have "Preserved our Glorious Union!" and that, in now paying the "National Debt," as they call it (as if the people themselves, ALL OF THEM WHO ARE TO BE TAXED FOR ITS PAYMENT, had really and voluntarily joined in contracting it), they are simply "Maintaining the National Honor!"

By "maintaining the national honor," they mean simply that they themselves, open robbers and murderers, assume to be the nation, and will keep faith with those who lend them the money necessary to enable them to crush the great body of the people under their feet; and will faithfully appropriate, from the proceeds of their future robberies and murders, enough to pay all their loans, principal and interest.

The pretense that the "abolition of slavery" was either a motive or justification for the war, is a fraud of the same character with that of "maintaining the national honor." Who, but such usurpers, robbers, and murderers as they, ever established slavery? Or what government, except one resting upon the sword, like the one we now have, was ever capable of maintaining slavery? And why did these men abolish slavery? Not from any love of liberty in general – not as an act of justice to the black man himself, but only "as a war measure," and because they wanted his assistance, and that of his friends, in carrying on the war they had undertaken for maintaining and intensifying that political, commercial, and industrial slavery, to which they have subjected the great body of the people, both black and white. And yet these imposters now cry out that they have abolished the chattel slavery of the black man – although that was not the motive of the war – as if they thought they could thereby conceal, atone for, or justify that other slavery which they were fighting to perpetuate, and to render more rigorous and inexorable than it ever was before. There was no difference of principle - but only of degree - between the slavery they boast they have abolished, and the slavery they were fighting to preserve; for all restraints upon men's natural liberty, not necessary for the simple maintenance of justice, are of the nature of slavery, and differ >from each other only in degree.

If their object had really been to abolish slavery, or maintain liberty or justice generally, they had only to say: All, whether white or black, who want the protection of this government, shall have it; and all who do not want it, will be left in peace, so long as they leave us in peace. Had they said this, slavery would necessarily have been abolished at once; the war would have been saved; and a thousand times nobler union than we have ever had would have been the result. It would have been a voluntary union of free men; such a union as will one day exist among all men, the world over, if the several nations, so called, shall ever get rid of the usurpers, robbers, and murderers, called governments, that now plunder, enslave, and destroy them.

Still another of the frauds of these men is, that they are now establishing, and that the war was designed to establish, "a government of consent." The only idea they have ever manifested as to what is a government of consent, is this - that it is one to which everybody must consent, or be shot. This idea was the dominant one on which the war was carried on; and it is the dominant one, now that we have got what is called "peace."

Their pretenses that they have "Saved the Country," and "Preserved our Glorious Union," are frauds like all the rest of their pretenses. By them they mean simply that they have subjugated, and maintained their power over, an unwilling people. This they call "Saving the Country"; as if an enslaved and subjugated people - or as if any people kept in subjection by the sword (as it is intended that all of us shall be hereafter) - could be said to have any country. This, too, they call "Preserving our Glorious Union"; as if there could be said to be any Union, glorious or inglorious, that was not voluntary. Or as if there could be said to be any union between masters and slaves; between those who conquer, and those who are subjugated.

All these cries of having "abolished slavery," of having "saved the country," of having "preserved the union," of establishing "a government of consent," and of "maintaining the national honor," are all gross, shameless, transparent cheats - so transparent that they ought to deceive no one - when uttered as justifications for the war, or for the government that has suceeded the war, or for now compelling the people to pay the cost of the war, or for compelling anybody to support a government that he does not want.

The lesson taught by all these facts is this: As long as mankind continue to pay "national debts," so-called - that is, so long as they are such dupes and cowards as to pay for being cheated, plundered, enslaved, and murdered - so long there will be enough to lend the money for those purposes; and with that money a plenty of tools, called soldiers, can be hired to keep them in subjection. But when they refuse any longer to pay for being thus cheated, plundered, enslaved, and murdered, they will cease to have cheats, and usurpers, and robbers, and murderers and blood-money loan-mongers for masters.

Appendix

In as much as the Constitution was never signed, nor agreed to, by anybody, as a contract, and therefore never bound anybody, and is now binding upon nobody; and is, moreover, such an one as no people can ever hereafter be expected to consent to, except as they may be forced to do so at the point of the bayonet, it is perhaps of no importance what its true legal meaning, as a contract, is. Nevertheless, the writer thinks it proper to say that, in his opinion, the Constitution is no such instrument as it has generally been assumed to be; but that by false interpretations, and naked usurpations, the government has been made in practice a very widely, and almost wholly, different thing from what the Constitution itself purports to authorize. He has heretofore written much, and could write much more, to prove that such is the truth. But whether the Constitution really be one thing, or another, this much is certain – that it has either authorized such a government as we have had, or has been powerless to prevent it. In either case, it is unfit to exist.

www.ReadHowYouWant.com

You can buy our **Large Type** and **EasyRead** books from our www.ReadHowYouWant.com website, from websites like Amazon.com and through your UK and North American bookshop.

EasyRead books are designed to make your reading easy and enjoyable. **EasyRead** books are published in different font sizes, so you can select the font size best for you.

EasyRead is for people with normal eyesight who want books in an easy-to-read format.

EasyRead Comfort is for people who find reading small print tiring but do not need large print.

EasyRead Large is for people who find it easier to read larger print.

The **EasyRead** font, character, word and line spacing have all been set to make it as easy as possible both to recognize a word, and to run your eye along a line of text without losing your place. We split as few words as possible at line ends, as split words make reading harder and can be annoying. For out-of-copyright books, words have been changed to modern spelling (where the sense is not affected), and the original hyphenation of compound words has been retained where this improves word recognition or sense.

With most things you buy, you get a choice, and you can choose the make and model that suits best. There is a big exception - books. You don't get to choose a format that is easy for you to read - you have to read the format the publisher selects.

This **"One Size Fits All"** paradigm **no longer** need apply to books.

At www.ReadHowYouWant.com, you can order a book just as you want it, so you can read it easily. You can choose nearly any format, and at a surprisingly low cost, because of a technical breakthrough that allows us to typeset an individual book automatically, print and bind the book and have it quickly sent directly to you.

You can have your book in **Talking Book** formats (**DAISY or MP3**) or as an **E-book** or in **Braille**.

We have developed totally new visual formats which we hope will help people with **dyslexia** and other print reading disabilities. Look at www.ReadHowYouWant.com for more information.

Made in the USA
Monee, IL
04 November 2026

67374659R00049